KINGDOM PRINCIPLES FOR EVERYDAY LIVING

40

Practical Principles for A Fruitful Life

Stewart B. Perrilliat

All scripture quotations herein are from the *King James*, the *Amplified*, the *New Living Translation*, or the *Message* versions of the Holy Bible.

KINGDOM PRINCIPLES FOR EVERYDAY LIVING:
40 Principles for a Fruitful Life

Stewart B. Perrilliat
P.O. Box 32785
San Jose, California 95152
1-888-972-9963
Website: www.kingdomfoundationrestorationcenter.com
Email: fruitfulliving@kingdomfoundationrestorationcenter.com

ISBN 978-0-9883918-1-9
Printed in the United States of America
Copyright © 2012 by Stewart B. Perrilliat

All rights reserved. No part of this book may be reproduced or transmitted in any form or by any means without written permission from the author.

Endorsements

My friend, Minister Stewart Perrilliat, has done a wonderful job of challenging us to develop and deploy our God-given gifts in accordance with our Maker's unique design for each of us. *Kingdom Principles for Everyday Living: 40 Practical Principles for a Fruitful Life* is a practical work that points us to the biblical blueprint for building a meaningful and rewarding life. This forty day devotional is a great way to invigorate and energize your day. Practice the timeless principles and strategies in this book and your understanding of God's plan for your life will be enriched!

Pastor Matt Anderson
Founder of Grace and Truth Ministries
President of Missing Peace Productions

Stewart B. Perrilliat's *Kingdom Principles for Everyday Living: 40 Practical Principles for a Fruitful Life* will challenge you to commit to the Kingdom of God daily living that will produce fruit of true repentance. The topics are relevant and the biblical context is well developed and I look forward to many testimonials of how this devotional has changed many lives.

Carey Ross,
Corporate Business Leader
President & CEO Principle Real Estate

Kingdom Principles for Everyday Living: 40 Practical Principles for a Fruitful Life is exactly what so many people need in their lives today: a practical road map that will lead you from a place of brokenness to a place of restoration and wholeness. Stewart's writings reflect who he is as a person: straightforward, sincere, encouraging, and loyal. Each daily reading gives readers a lesson that will help them apply God's wisdom to their lives and overcome the struggles that hinder so many of us in today's challenging times. It is my pleasure to recommend this book.

Rufus Chambers
Entrepreneur & Ministry Leader

It gives me great pleasure to recommend *Kingdom Principles for Everyday Living: 40 Practical Principles for a Fruitful Life* to anyone who has a desire to build a strong foundation for his or her life. God has used Stewart as His anointed scribe to pen a book that has at its foundation the application of "principles." Principles are the currency of life. They have value around the world. It doesn't matter what country you find yourself in, real principles can be applied right where you are. *Kingdom Principles for Everyday Living* is a great tool that everyone will benefit from and keep them on track to spiritual maturity. One of the most powerful principles can be found on day seventeen. If you master this one, you are well on your way to success in life.

Kingdom Principles for Everyday Living: 40 Practical Principles for a Fruitful Life gives you an opportunity to invest in the most important person in the world, you!

Robert Edward
Edward Ministries International
Global Physical Security Account Manager

Acknowledgments

I would like to thank the following people for the assistance, encouragement, enthusiasm, and support given to me during the writing of this book. In no particular order they are: Matt and Kem Anderson, Jackie Seeno, Cy Forth, Rufus Chambers, Karla Allen, Helyn Manning, Kimberly Allen, Stephanie Jackson, Erica Benjamin, and Kimra Elliot.

To Pastor J. Alfred Sr., my childhood mentor, thank you for your continued encouragement and support throughout my adult life.

Dedication

I take this opportunity to first thank God for the gift to pen His inspiration that the world may read, be encouraged, edified, and empowered in these last days.

I dedicate this book to my three amazing children Jessica, Stewart, Jr., and Destiny. Through life's storms and battles, you are Daddy's pride and joy. Your smiles have brought me motivation to pursue my dreams and fulfill my purpose here on Earth. Thank you for your unconditional love and support. As you go after your dreams in life, may God bless each of you. Love Always!!!

Finally, to my mother Sarah Elizabeth who has been a rock in my life. Thank you for your wisdom, love, and unending support. Love you!

Table of Contents

Preface		10
Introduction		12
Day 1	Check Your Heart	14
Day 2	Repentance	18
Day 3	Never Give Up	22
Day 4	Born into Sin	24
Day 5	God is Calling You	26
Day 6	Serving a Perfect God	28
Day 7	The Lord's Promise	30
Day 8	God Will Guide You	32
Day 9	God's Way is Perfect	34
Day 10	The Kingdom is Different	36
Day 11	Who is with You?	38
Day 12	Jesus is Praying for You	40
Day 13	The Name	44
Day 14	God is on Your Side	46
Day 15	The Enemy Wants You Dead	48
Day 16	Seek the Lord	50
Day 17	Love Your Enemies	52
Day 18	Perfect and Complete in Him	56
Day 19	The Setup	58
Day 20	Who Created Who?	60
Day 21	God is Demanding All of You	62

Day 22	The Eternal Living God	64
Day 23	Jesus is the Light of the World	66
Day 24	Put Away Childish Things	68
Day 25	God is the Source of Your Every Need	70
Day 26	The Battle Belongs to God	72
Day 27	Creating Wealth is Not a Mystery	76
Day 28	God is Everything	78
Day 29	Comfort During Your Time of Mourning	80
Day 30	Your Greatest Weapon is Love	84
Day 31	What is Salvation?	88
Day 32	Faith Being Tested	90
Day 33	Who are You?	94
Day 34	A Healthy Body and a Prosperous Soul	96
Day 35	Do Not Blame God	98
Day 36	Give God Praise and Rejoice	102
Day 37	You Have Been Chosen by God	106
Day 38	Are You Really Born Again?	110
Day 39	Get in the Game	114
Day 40	Turning Toward God	118

Preface

Every Christian should grow in his or her relationship with Christ. Through thoughtful reflections, based on scriptural principles, a believer's life matures and produces a fruitful life. A fruitful life is a happy and balanced life. Reading *Kingdom Principles for Everyday Living* by Stewart Perrilliat is an excellent way to begin and continue walking the paths for fruitful living.

Stewart is highly qualified as a Christian writer. I have known him since he was five years old. He has always been a person of integrity. God has always had a serious claim upon his life. In 1997, Brother Perrilliat and I traveled to the Holy Land together. While there we studied the sacred scriptures in their biblical, historical, theological, and social setting. If anyone has a clear vision of practical principles for a fruitful life, it is Stewart Perrilliat. I am happy because of our relationships in the Gospel and because it is a joy to commend his excellent book to you.

You may use this book to enhance your daily devotional life. You may also use this book for study in small group Bible study, or for home Bible studies. You should find this book useful at church retreats and conferences. You will discover that this book will also be useful in helping you to introduce Jesus Christ to non-Christians. In fact, I encourage you to purchase copies of this book as a gift to friends.

J. Alfred Smith, Sr.
Pastor Emeritus of Allen Temple Baptist Church
Oakland, California
Distinguished professor of Preaching and Church Ministries
American Baptist Seminary of the West
Berkeley, California

Introduction

Over the years, I have come to understand the significance of the number 40. Scientifically speaking, 40 weeks is the length of time it takes for a mother to carry an unborn child from conception to delivery. Biblically speaking, 40 is the number associated with a period of testing before a breakthrough.

The number 40 is an indication that God is ready to birth something new out of pain or challenge. According to the Bible, Noah was in the rain for 40 days and nights before God brought a refreshing promise for His people.

When the Children of Israel were ready to cross over into their promise, the spies who preceded them took 40 days to scout out the land. However, because of disobedience, their 40 days turned into 40 years before they entered into the land of promise.

Goliath, who was killed by David, challenged the Children of Israel for 40 days prior to their victory over the Philistine army.

Before He began His ministry, Jesus, while being tempted by satan, fasted for 40 days and 40 nights in the wilderness.

I have experienced my own personal 40 days of trials and tribulations. However, because I did not lose my confidence in God, I was able to realize the significance of the number 40 and receive God's blessings for me after my test. These truths concerning the number 40 inspired me to write this devotional.

In modern times, 30 days is used to complete various programs or to create a new habit. At the beginning of the year, Magazine cover stories often read, *Thirty Days to a New You*. For the purpose of this devotional the true number for the manifestation of a renewed life is the number 40.

Therefore, this devotional will afford you an opportunity to develop a more intimate relationship with the Lord and transform your life. As you read this devotional, it will give you hope and renew your strength. On those days when doubt and disbelief abound, I encourage you to remain consistent with your 40 day cycle of reading *Kingdom Principles for Everyday Living: 40 Practical Principals for a Fruitful Life*.

I challenge you to apply yourself and expect a breakthrough by the time you have complete this devotional. I encourage you to not only read through the devotions in this book, but to read the related scriptures and commit them to memory. This process will increase your knowledge of God, and strengthen your faith towards Him.

God's will for us is to increase in every area of our lives by being doers of His Word. I pray that this devotional draw you closer to God and give you the incredible power to break into your promise.

-Stewart Perrilliat

Day 1

Check Your Heart

My God! I've had it with them! Blow them away! Tumbleweeds in the desert waste, charred sticks in the burned-over ground. Knock the breath right out of them, so they're gasping for breath, gasping, "God." Bring them to the end of their rope, and leave them there dangling, helpless. Then they'll learn your name: "God," the one and only High God on earth. (Psalm 83:13-18 MSG)

Oftentimes we find ourselves in situations just like King David in Psalm 83. Although we do not fight a physical battle, the spiritual battle, which occurs in the invisible realm, is just as intense. Nevertheless, notice that David was secure enough in His relationship with God to call his enemies God's enemies. King David is saying, "God, do whatever You need to do, even to the point of hurting them, if necessary."

Do you ever wonder what this "God walk" is all about? Is it really about Christianity or is it about the Kingdom lifestyle? Living a Kingdom lifestyle requires you to have a personal relationship with Jesus Christ. He must first be the Lord of your life.

Some people believe that Jesus existed historically. Others, who live a Kingdom lifestyle, believe that Jesus lives in their hearts, and they allow that conviction to govern every aspect of their lives. Be honest. Is Jesus the Lord of your life? Is your relationship about tradition or is it about revelation? Is it about getting spiritually high without authentic transformation or is it about God who is the Most High?

Take time to meditate on the Word of God today and see if your life resembles the world's standards or God's standards. Look into the "mirror" and evaluate yourself. Ask God to reveal the necessary adjustments you need to make in your life. Pray that God will show you how to make the changes to become exactly who and what God has purposely designed. Then, you can become like David and call your enemies God's enemies.

Share some light in this dark world.

Practical Application for Kingdom Living

Each day, perform a heart test to see where you are with God. Allow the Holy Spirit to assess your heart-health. Write down what He shows you and make the necessary adjustments to have a heart that is right before God.

Kingdom Principles for Everyday Living

Day 2

Repentance

When the cool evening breezes were blowing, the man and his wife heard the LORD God walking about in the garden. So they hid from the LORD God among the trees. Then the LORD God called to the man, "Where are you?" He replied, "I heard you walking in the garden, so I hid. I was afraid because I was naked." (Genesis 3:8-10 NLT)

God was not asking Adam where he was geographically; He already knew where he was. God was asking him where he was spiritually, because He knew Adam's actions produced spiritual death.

After Adam had eaten the forbidden fruit in the Garden of Eden, he heard God walking in the garden. Because his actions produced guilt and shame, he hid from God. When you disobey God, you begin to die spiritually, just like Adam. As a result of sin, you are separated from God, who is your life source.

Instead of hiding from Him, God is asking you to come to Him and acknowledge your mistakes. Take some time and confess what you have done wrong, and God will remove your guilt and shame through the blood of Christ. Tell Him you are sorry for the sins you have committed knowingly and unknowingly. When you change your heart, mind, and direction, God will respond to you favorably.

If we confess our sins, He is faithful and just to forgive us our sins, and to cleanse us from all unrighteousness (1 John 1:9 KJV).

You are not waiting on God to make the changes in your life. God is waiting on you.

A Kingdom lifestyle requires true repentance.

Kingdom Principles for Everyday Living

Practical Application for Kingdom Living

Write down the thoughts and actions you need to confess to God and repent of them. Today, start building a solid foundation and Kingdom lifestyle through God.

Kingdom Principles for Everyday Living

Day 3

Never Give Up

So let's not get tired of doing what is good. At just the right time we will reap a harvest of blessing if we do not give up. (Galatians 6:9 NLT)

As for the rest of you, dear brothers and sisters, never get tired of doing good. (2 Thessalonians 3:13 NLT)

Have you ever asked yourself these questions? Why does everyone appear to be blessed except me? When will my blessings appear? How is it that I pay my tithes and give my offerings every paycheck, and I am barely making it? Even though I sow my time and talents in the Kingdom of God, why am I doing worse than the unbeliever who does not even know You?

Some people are blessed because they simply follow Kingdom principles. Oftentimes, we lack insight regarding the length of time a person has waited and what has transpired in their life in order to receive their current blessings.

God is simply saying, "Keep doing what you are doing, and do not give up. I have not forgotten you, and I will bless you at the appointed time."

God knows what He has promised you, and at the right time, He will open up the Heavens for you and pour out blessings that you won't have room to contain. Listen, God is saying, "Do not give up and do not give in because your blessings are sure." Be encouraged and know that God has not forgotten you.

Practical Application for Kingdom Living

Giving up is not an option with God. If you think you cannot make it, take a few moments and tell God how you feel. Believe it or not, He is concerned with everything about you. He cares about where you are and He will empower you to endure until your blessings manifest.

Day 4

Born into Sin

I have discovered this principle of life—that when I want to do what is right, I inevitably do what is wrong. (Romans 7:21 NLT)

Have you ever felt when you wanted to do right, you found yourself doing wrong? In *Romans 7,* the Apostle Paul talks about the struggle to do what is right or wrong. According to Paul, the war between the flesh and the spirit was constantly at work inside of him.

The Bible says, *"A righteous man falls seven times and rises again..."* (*Proverbs 24:16 AMP*). It is not a man's failures that make him righteous, but his ability to get up. Today, I encourage you not to give up. You are destined for greatness if you continue and do not give up.

When the Second Adam, Jesus Christ, was born, He paid the full price to redeem you. *"...He that knew no sin became sin..."* (*2 Corinthians 5:21 KJV*). Always remember, *"...Greater is He that is in me,* which is Jesus Christ, *than He that is in the world"* (*1 John 4:4 NLT*). Since you are in Christ, victory belongs to you. In the end, you win!

Practical Application for Kingdom Living

Take a few moments to allow the Holy Spirit to show you why you continue to struggle in certain areas. Write down and study the scriptures that will help strengthen you in these areas. Lastly, find another believer that will pray with you and keep you accountable in this area.

Day 5

God is Calling You

Go through, go through the gates; prepare ye the way of the people; cast up, cast up the highway; gather out the stones; lift up a standard for the people (Isaiah 62:10 KJV).

God is not a spare tire to be pulled out whenever you get a flat tire only to be thrown back into the trunk until the next time you need Him. God is calling you to a higher standard and level of dedication. Are you ready and are you willing to take the journey?

Today, make a covenant with God—a promise between the two of you. Let Him know that you are willing to commit to the standard He requires. Tell Him, "God, all I need to know is You are calling me, and I will come."

It is God's way or no way.

Practical Application for Kingdom Living

Today is the day for you to come into agreement with God's promises and purposes for your life. Write down the steps you need to take in order to reach the highest level of Kingdom living.

Day 6

Serving a Perfect God

And we know that God causes everything to work together for the good of those who love God and are called according to his purpose for them.
(Romans 8:28 NLT)

God knows every plan for your life because He is the creator of everything. Nothing in life just happens. There is a purpose for everything we encounter in life. *Romans 8:28* makes it clear. If we love Him and keep working toward perfection in Him, God will use all of our experiences to fulfill His purpose through us.

Do you love God? Are you called according to His purpose? If this describes you, then you qualify for the grand prize that God will reveal in time.

As for God, His way is perfect. The Word of the LORD is tried: He is a buckler to all of them that trust in Him.
(2 Samuel 22:31 KJV)

Practical Application for Kingdom Living

According to God's purpose for your life, I challenge you today to write down three specific areas God wants to perfect in you.

_____
_____
_____
_____
_____
_____
_____
_____
_____
_____
_____
_____
_____
_____
_____
_____
_____
_____
_____
_____
_____
_____
_____
_____
_____

Day 7

The Lord's Promise

> *While Jeremiah was still confined in the courtyard of the guard, the Lord gave him this second message: "This is what the Lord says—the Lord who made the earth, who formed and established it, whose name is the Lord: Ask me and I will tell you remarkable secrets you do not know about things to come.(Jeremiah 33:1-3 NLT)*

I once heard a Christian say: "If you lived through circumstances that should have killed you, it qualifies and empowers you to help others." Is it your testimony that you are only here by the grace of God?

God has a purpose and a plan for your life. His plan is to restore you to His original intent for your life. All you have to do is simply call Him. In essence, capture God's attention. One way you attract His attention is by conversing with Him as you would with others you know. God yearns to speak with you on a daily basis.

God promises to show you great and mighty things. Ask God to show you what He has planned for your life.

Pray to Him saying, "God show me the unsearchable things you promised me, and bring restoration to my life." Call out to Him today and watch Him answer you, because it is a promise straight from the throne room of Heaven.

I declare your latter days will be greater than your former days.

Practical Application for Kingdom Living

I encourage you to ask God to show you all of the hidden treasures He sees concerning you. As God begins to unfold the mysteries of your life, start writing them down as He gives them to you and believe they will manifest in your life.

_____
_____
_____
_____
_____
_____
_____
_____
_____
_____
_____
_____
_____
_____
_____
_____
_____
_____
_____
_____

Day 8

God Will Guide You

> *The LORD went ahead of them. He guided them during the day with a pillar of cloud, and he provided light at night with a pillar of fire. This allowed them to travel by day or by night.*
> *(Exodus 13:21 NLT)*

The LORD went ahead of the Children of Israel, guiding them during the day with a pillar of cloud, and providing light at night with a pillar of fire. The pillar of cloud and the pillar of fire were the Children of Israel's "navigation system."

God was with them and carried them the entire way. Yet, they neither knew Him nor trusted Him. What good is a navigation system, if you do not know how to properly use it?

This same concept applies to the Bible. What good is the Word of God, if you do not trust what it says or know how to use it? The Word of God is your navigation system. It is available to guide you to your destination. Follow God's Word and His directions and He will lead you to your "promised land."

> *"Trust in the Lord with all thine heart; and lean not unto thine own understanding. In all thy ways acknowledge Him, and He shall direct thy paths."*
> *(Proverbs 3:5-6 KJV)*

Practical Application for Kingdom Living

Where is God leading you today? I encourage you to write down five things you trust and believe God to accomplish for you, so you can reach your "promised land."

_____
_____
_____
_____
_____
_____
_____
_____
_____
_____
_____
_____
_____
_____
_____
_____
_____
_____
_____
_____

Day 9

God's Way is Perfect

God's way is perfect. All the Lord's promises prove true. He is a shield for all who look to him for protection. (Psalm 18:30 NLT)

We all go through dry seasons in our lives where we feel all alone. As time continues to pass, we may get frustrated and want to give up. We might even question God and His ways. Do not think for one second God has forgotten you. You may not be where you want to be in life, but that does not mean God has abandoned you. God said, "*...He will never leave you nor forsake you*" *(Hebrews 13:5 KJV)*.

You serve a perfect God. He does not make mistakes. However, God is not on man's timetable. He is on a divine clock and a divine timetable. You have to come to a point in your life where you can honestly tell God, "I do not understand what You are doing, but I believe You are making the best decisions for my life because Your ways are perfect."

Trust the Lord today. He will protect you as He perfects you, because He is your shield.

Practical Application for Kingdom Living

I encourage you to write down your frustrations and those moments when you have felt abandoned. Afterwards, pray and ask God to help strengthen your faith. Then allow the peace of God to regulate and control your heart as He perfects all things concerning you.

_____
_____
_____
_____
_____
_____
_____
_____
_____
_____
_____
_____
_____
_____
_____
_____
_____
_____
_____
_____
_____
_____

Day 10

The Kingdom is Different

But many are the greatest now will be least important then, and those who seem least important now will be the greatest then. (Matthew 19:30 NLT)

But those who exalt themselves will be humbled and those who humble themselves will be exalted. (Matthew 23:12 NLT)

It is amazing that the Kingdom of God is so different from the world's standards. In the world, everyone wants to be first, however, the Word of God says, *"...the first will be last and the last will be first" (Matthew 19:30 NLT)*.

Everyone wants to know, "What is in it for me?" Sometimes, even Christians feel a sense of entitlement. On the other hand, the real church experience is not about what you can get, but rather, what God can get from you. But the Word says, *"...it is better to give than to receive" (Acts 20:35 NLT)*. In other words, what are you giving God?

We all want to be served, but this is a backwards approach in the Kingdom. Jesus Christ was a servant until the day of His death. In a world where people hate each other, the Bible still says, *"...love is the greatest gift of all" (1 Corinthians 13:13 NLT)*.

Practical Application for Kingdom Living

Is your life a part of the Kingdom or the world? I encourage you to take some time and allow the Holy Spirit to examine your heart. Write down those areas where you need help converting your life from the world's standards to the Kingdom's standards. Then ask God to help you make the adjustments.

_____
_____
_____
_____
_____
_____
_____
_____
_____
_____
_____
_____
_____
_____
_____
_____
_____
_____

Day 11

Who is with You?

I have told you all this so that you may have peace in me. Here on earth you will have many trials and sorrows. But take heart, because I have overcome the world. (John 16:33 NLT)

Due to the nation's unstable economy, it has become increasingly more difficult to acquire the basic necessities in life. Nevertheless, the God we serve is El Shaddai—The Almighty One.

As the youngest of three boys growing up in some of the roughest areas in East Oakland, California, maintaining a sense of peace was easier said than done. Nonetheless, the peace I had was the assurance that God would take care of me. I was confident if anything occurred, God would get involved.

In *John 16:33*, God is giving us a preview about what to expect in this world, and He wants to assure us that we will have peace in Him regardless of the adversities we may face. God is saying, "I will be there for you!"

I want to encourage you today to set your eyes upon Him, because God has power over everything in this world. The Bible says, *"If God is for you, then who can be against you?"* (see Romans 8:31). Do not forget who is with you!

Practical Application for Kingdom Living

Take some time and think about all the distractions and setbacks in your life that caused you to doubt God, and then begin to write them down. Next, ask God for the direction and wisdom necessary to accomplish His plan for your life.

_____
_____
_____
_____
_____
_____
_____
_____
_____
_____
_____
_____
_____
_____
_____
_____
_____
_____
_____
_____

Day 12

Jesus is Praying for You

Simon, Simon, satan has asked to sift each of you like wheat. But I have pleaded in prayer for you, Simon, that your faith should not fail. So when you have repented and turned to me again, strengthen your brothers. (Luke 22:31-32 NLT)

In this scripture, Jesus is talking to Simon Peter. Jesus is warning Peter that the enemy wants to separate him from Jesus. Jesus knows that Peter is going to mess up and turn from Him, just like He knows that about you.

Jesus knows how important it is to pray, because He understands satan's ultimate goal is to steal, kill, and destroy. If Peter did not go through the time of testing, it would have been difficult for Him to witness to others and preach with great power and authority.

How can you be effective for the Kingdom of God if you have not been through the fire? How can you encourage others to make a fresh start if you have not experienced it for yourself?

Satan will try his best to separate you from God. He will try to abort every prophecy, promise, and purpose God has preordained for your life. Just as Jesus prayed for Peter, you have the assurance that He is interceding for you. In order for you to become as pure as gold, God will allow you to be tested, tried, and proven (see *Job 23:10*). When you are proven, you can tell others about God's goodness and mercy.

Always remember, satan's desire is to take, eradicate and devastate your life. When I was ignorant of the things of God, in the same manner Jesus prayed for Peter, Jesus, and many others, prayed for me. I share the Word the way I do because apart from prayer, I would never be where I am today. I encourage you to pray every day and ask the Lord to order your steps and guide your every decision. *We overcome by the blood of the Lamb and the word of our testimony...* (see *Revelation 12:11*).

When we are strong in the Lord and fully converted, then we need to go back and strengthen our brothers and sisters in the Lord

Practical Application for Kingdom Living

Take a moment and write down the names of those who you know are going through serious trials. Then, pray that God will help them on their journey to restoration and freedom.

Kingdom Principles for Everyday Living

Day 13

The Name

Therefore, God elevated him to the place of highest honor and gave him the name above all other names. (Philippians 2:9 NLT)

The Bible says, God has highly exalted Jesus and given Him the name that is above every name. We wrestle against many names such as cancer, poverty, drugs, alcohol, terrible bosses, religion, and even contrary loved ones. No matter what it is, if it has a name, the name of Jesus is above that name. Therefore, when you use the name of Jesus, you begin to cancel every other name and operate in extraordinary power.

There is wonderworking power in the name of Jesus. If you are tired of trying to do things on your own, begin to operate in the supernatural power that is available to every believer through the name of Jesus.

When you accept Jesus Christ as your Lord and Savior, you inherit supernatural power. When you begin operating in the supernatural, you are no longer depending on your own natural ability, but you operate in the supernatural power that exists in the name of Jesus Christ.

That at the name of Jesus every knee should bow, of things in heaven, and things in earth, and things under the earth; And that every tongue should confess that Jesus Christ is Lord, to the glory of God the Father. (Philippians 2:10-11 KJV)

Practical Application for Kingdom Living

Is there anything in your life that has gone beyond your ability to fix? I encourage you to write those situations down and pray using the authority found in the name of Jesus and watch Him exceed your greatest expectations.

_____
_____
_____
_____
_____
_____
_____
_____
_____
_____
_____
_____
_____
_____
_____
_____
_____
_____
_____
_____

Day 14

God is on Your Side

Many evils confront the [consistently] righteous, but the Lord delivers him out of them all.
(Psalm 34:19 AMP)

Have you ever thought, "Wow, just when I started living for God, all hell broke loose?" Could it be because satan is no longer your partner and now he feels that you have betrayed him? You left him to serve God.

There was a time when you were serving the adversary, the devil. At one point in your life, you and satan were partners in sin. He knew you were on his side and he could count on you whenever he needed you. Now, even though, you are serving God Almighty, you find yourself in a fight every day.

If your adversary, satan, is not attacking you today, then perhaps you are not a threat to him. God wants you to know that no matter how much you are attacked by your enemy, with God on your side, you cannot lose. If he knocks all the air out of you, leaving you breathless, you can whisper a prayer and God will hear it. God wants you to know He is as near to you as a whispered prayer, and He will come and deliver you from the hands of your enemies every time.

You have to know for yourself that God is on your side.

Practical Application for Kingdom Living

I encourage you today to write down your prayer requests and begin to pray to God about them, and never forget," God is on your side."

Day 15

The Enemy Wants You Dead

The thief's purpose is to steal and kill and destroy. My purpose is to give them a rich and satisfying life.
(John 10:10 NLT)

Whether we know it or not, we all have experienced close encounters with death. There are things that happen in the spirit realm unbeknownst to us, but God is there protecting us. He dispatches His angels all around us throughout our lives. Because God has a plan and purpose for our lives, only He knows when it is our time to die.

It would be unfortunate to die before living out your true purpose in life. Jesus did not die for you so you can live haphazardly. When He died for you, He gave you the provision for an abundant life. Jesus said, *I have come so that you can have life and life more abundantly (John 10:10 KJV).*

Today, I challenge you to stop looking at your problems or your past and focus your eyes on Him. Always remember, He paid the price for you to live and not die.

Practical Application for Kingdom Living

Take some time to meditate on this Word and reflect on those times when God preserved your life. Write down all of your close encounters with death. Whether it was a health issue or car accident, begin to pray and thank God for His mercy and grace that saved your life.

Day 16

Seek the Lord

Seek the LORD while you can find him. Call on him now while he is near. (Isaiah 55:6 KJV)

Have you ever found it difficult to believe God is near when you need Him? Have you ever searched for God only to feel empty and incomplete? You may have said, "I know He exists, but I just cannot hear Him." In your desperation, you may have found yourself saying, "God, if you do this, then I will do that." Still, all you hear is silence.

Deuteronomy 4:29 (AMP) says, "But if from there you will seek (inquire for and require as necessity) the Lord your God, you will find Him if you [truly] seek Him with all your heart [and mind] and soul and life."

Regardless of your circumstances or your feelings, if you search for Him with all your heart, mind, and soul, you will find Him. *God is a rewarder of those that diligently seek Him* (see Hebrews 11:6 KLV).

Practical Application for Kingdom Living

Write down the things you need God to do in your life today. Once this is done, ask Him to give you the steps to achieve these goals.

Day 17

Love Your Enemies

You have heard the law that says, 'Love your neighbor' and hate your enemy. But I say, love your enemies! Pray for those who persecute you! In that way, you will be acting as true children of your Father in heaven. For He gives His sunlight to both the evil and the good, and He sends rain on the just and the unjust alike. If you love only those who love you, what reward is there for that? Even corrupt tax collectors do that much. If you are kind only to your friends, how are you different from anyone else? Even pagans do that. But you are to be perfect, even as your Father in heaven is perfect. (Matthew 5:43-48 NLT)

We say we want to be Christ-like, that is, until we get treated like Christ. God will allow us to go through things that are beyond our control and use those things to help build character.

It is possible to praise God when we have been persecuted, lied on, and even betrayed. It is during these times that we are forced to go the extra mile, even when we do not feel like it. We keep trying, because we understand that God will complete the work He started in us.

It seems as if those who are closest to us are oftentimes the ones who hurt us the most. *Luke 6:27-28*, says, *But to you who are willing to listen, I say, love your enemies! Do good to those who hate you. Bless those who curse you. Pray for those who hurt you.*

When we speak about these things, we have to ask the question, who is the stronger person; the one who acts out through emotions, or the one who relies on the strength of God? We must look to Jesus who led by example. Do you remember when Jesus was on the cross? He said,

"Father, forgive them for they know not what they are doing (Luke 23:34 NLT). He was praying for those who were persecuting Him.

We must let God be our example of how to love our enemies. Even when we were not living for God, He still loved us enough to send His only son, Jesus, to die for us. Yes, He died for us because He loved us *(John 3:16 NLT)*. God already knew we would live outside of His will, and yet, He still sent his Son to die for us. This whole scripture is saying, when we operate in this kind of love, then we are operating as true children of our Father in Heaven. Wow, what a challenging word for us to live by.

If we are kind only to our friends, how are we different from anyone else? Even unbelievers do that. But, we are to be perfect, even as our Father in heaven is perfect.

Practical Application for Kingdom Living

Who has mistreated or offended you? Write down their names, make a decision to forgive and pray for them. Your obedience will release Kingdom benefits.

Kingdom Principles for Everyday Living

Day 18

Perfect and Complete in Him

You want what you do not have, so you scheme and kill to get it. You are jealous of what others have, but you cannot get it, so you fight and wage war to take it away from them. Yet, you do not have what you want because you do not ask God for it. (James: 4:2 NLT)

When we look at our lives, we may feel inadequate because of all the wrong things we have done prior to accepting Christ. However, when we give our lives totally to Jesus, we are complete in Him. We are perfect in God's eyes because of the blood of Jesus.

In the book of James, we are encouraged to count trouble as an opportunity to rejoice, because we know when we are tested, our spiritual muscles are exercised. We must continue to exercise our faith with joy, because when our endurance is fully developed, then we are made perfect and complete in Him—nothing missing, nothing broken, and nothing lacking in our lives. God wants us all to be perfect and complete in Him.

Kingdom Principles for Everyday Living

Practical Application for Kingdom Living

God has forgiven you and if you are born again, then you are complete in Him. Albeit true, perhaps you have not forgiven yourself. Write down the things you have not forgiven yourself for, and then release those things to God and trust that the blood of Christ has done a complete work to make certain you are free and complete in Him.

_____
_____
_____
_____
_____
_____
_____
_____
_____
_____
_____
_____
_____
_____
_____

Day 19

The Setup

> *Dear brothers and sisters, when troubles come your way, consider it an opportunity for great joy. For you know that when your faith is tested, your endurance has a chance to grow. So let it grow, for when your endurance is fully developed, you will be perfect and complete, needing nothing. (James 1:2-4 NLT)*

Trying times will cause us to pray for things we would not typically request. However, God knows our needs better than we do. Understanding difficult times are used to manifest God's plan for our lives, gives us the assurance that our lives always fall into alignment with His will no matter what we go through. This is an important key to surviving some of life's frustrations.

We all have had times when we prayed, "Lord give me patience to get through this." Little did we know when we prayed for patience, we prayed for the trying of our faith. Paul gives us specific instructions for success when our faith is tried. When we rejoice through our trials and allow patience to do a complete work in us, we are brought to a place of maturity in the Kingdom.

Practical Application for Kingdom Living

Meditate on the scripture, *James 1:2-8*. Next, write down your prayer request. Finally, rejoice and allow the fruit of the spirit to manifest as patience in your life.

Day 20

Who Created Who

God is not a man, so he does not lie. He is not human, so he does not change his mind. Has he ever spoken and failed to act? Has he ever promised and not carried it through? (Numbers 23:19 NLT)

In spite of your faults, imperfections, and inadequacies, you are who God says you are. Oftentimes, people may label you and place a brand on you. Truthfully, people cannot dictate your destiny nor can they tell you the purpose of your true existence on Earth. Since man did not make you, then man does not have the answers or solutions to your problems unless God chooses to reveal it to him.

God created everything. He created you and has a master plan for your life. As you seek Him, He will show you, in depth, the destiny for your life.

Our lives do not always seem to align with who God says we are, but if God said it, we must believe it, and that settles it! Remember, you are who God says you are.

Practical Application for Kingdom Living

Mediate on this scripture, *Numbers 23:19*. Then write down those things God has said and is saying about you. Finally, pray, and believe that what you have prayed for, God has already done!

_____
_____
_____
_____
_____
_____
_____
_____
_____
_____
_____
_____
_____
_____
_____
_____
_____
_____
_____
_____

Day 21

God is Demanding All of You

For whoever is bent on saving his [temporal] life [his comfort and security here] shall lose it [eternal life]; and whoever loses his life [his comfort and security here] for My sake shall find it [life everlasting]. (Matthew 16:25 AMP)

Did you know we are only passing through this life on Earth? When we understand we are here temporarily, we will begin to take life more seriously. This life is only preparing us for the day we will see Christ face to face. However, we have to give up our lives in order to gain everlasting life. I know that may sound strange or backwards, but this is a prerequisite to receiving eternal life. Eternal life, life after death, allows you to live in eternity forever. In other words, you will never die.

Whoever gives up their life for Christ, receives eternal life. Today, give it up. To live is Christ and to die is gain *(see Philippians 1:21 KJV)*.

Practical Application for Kingdom Living

What is it that you need to give up in order to fulfill the purpose of God? Write those things down and then pray and ask God to help you to die to your flesh, so you may be alive to God through Christ.

Day 22

The Eternal Living God

In the beginning the Word already existed. The Word was with God, and the Word was God.
(John 1:1 NLT)

People serve all kinds of gods. A god is anything you give your highest devotion, adoration and attention to as to make it an idol. Your wife, husband and even your kids can be your god. Your job can be your god too. Even your nice house or special edition car can be your god. Any idol you worship becomes your god.

What makes Christianity different from any other religion? We do not worship inanimate objects or humans. We worship the only, true, living, and eternal God.

Christianity is the only religion that has observed and continues to see prophecies spoken over thousands of years ago, come to pass. No book has ever been written with the insight, wisdom and revelation contained within the pages of the Holy Bible, this is true because God and His Word are one.

Today, I encourage you to pick up your Bible and begin your devotion with *John 1:1*.

Practical Application for Kingdom Living

I encourage you to be honest with yourself and list those things you have placed above God. Then, repent, make a fresh commitment to worship the only true and living God, and make Him your priority.

Day 23

Jesus is the Light of the World

satan, who is the god of this world, has blinded the minds of those who do not believe. They are unable to see the glorious light of the Good News. They do not understand this message about the glory of Christ, who is the exact likeness of God.
(2 Corinthians 4:4 NLT)

The world is a dark place, and everything evil is done in darkness. How can we live in darkness and expect to see clearly? It is not until we truly invite Christ into our hearts that we begin to see the true light. Jesus said, *"...I am the light of the world (John 8:12 KJV),* and it is hard to understand what that means if you are not a believer.

The Bible was not written for nonbelievers and those living in darkness, but for those in the true light. If you are tired of living in darkness and you need some light in your life, ask God for a fresh revelation concerning the Word of God. The Bible says, *"Ask and you shall receive, seek and you shall find, knock and the door shall open unto you (Matthew 7:7 KJV).* ASK!

Practical Application for Kingdom Living

Write down the areas where you need the light of God to shine. Then, allow the light of His Word to transform those areas.

Day 24

Put Away Childish Things

When I was a child, I spoke and thought and reasoned as a child. But when I grew up, I put away childish things. (1 Corinthians 13:11 NLT)

There comes a time when we need to change the way we do things in life. When we were children, our excuse was we did not know better. However, there comes a time when we can no longer remain in the same place. We have to shift into drive and accelerate into the destiny God has predestined for our lives.

Just as we expect our natural children to grow into productive adults, as Kingdom children of God, we are also expected to consistently mature in every area of our lives

When we initially gave our lives to Jesus Christ, immaturity was expected. However, as we grow, we are shaped into the image of God, so that our spiritual maturity is evident to all.

If we want the things of God, then we have to start living according to the Word of God. I want to encourage you today to list five things you need to change in your life in order to mature in God. Pray over those things and tell God you want to put away childish things and remove them from your life forever. I guarantee you; God will meet you right where you are. God is waiting for you today.

Practical Application for Kingdom Living

List five areas where you need God to help you mature.

Day 25

God is the Source of Your Every Need

And this same God who takes care of me will supply all your needs from his glorious riches, which have been given to us in Christ Jesus. (Philippians 4:19 NLT)

Everyone has a need and God has promised to provide those needs. When you need electricity, in order to get power, you must first find a source to plug into. God is your power source. If you have a need, then God has a supply for your every need.

Express to God exactly what you need. Do not forget to remind God what He has promised in His Word. Tell God, "I know what Your Word says and I am praying to You today according to *Philippians 4:19*. I am a child of God, I am a giver, I am a tither, and I am a citizen of the Kingdom of God."

Begin to declare and decree your needs are met according to the Word of God. Amen!

Practical Application for Kingdom Living

Write down exactly what you need and begin to declare that your needs are met according to the Word of God in Jesus Name.

_____
_____
_____
_____
_____
_____
_____
_____
_____
_____
_____
_____
_____
_____
_____
_____
_____
_____
_____
_____
_____
_____

Day 26

The Battle Belongs to God

He said, Hearken, all Judah, you inhabitants of Jerusalem, and you King Jehoshaphat. The Lord says this to you: Be not afraid or dismayed at this great multitude; for the battle is not yours, but God's. (2 Chronicles 20:15 AMP)

There comes a time in life when you have to know who is fighting your battles. Oftentimes you may face intimidating battles that threaten to swallow you up and spit you out. However, you have to hear the voice of God, through His Word, telling you not to be afraid.

Remember, no matter how enormous your battle is today, it is not yours. The battle belongs to God! As long as you attempt to fight your own conflict, it will seem impossible. However, when you release it to God, you will experience true victory. God wants to remove it more than you do, but He refuses to do anything as long as you have your hands on it. God is a perfect gentleman, and He will not force Himself on you.

Trust me; God wants to help you. But, it must be on His terms and conditions. Give Him the opportunity to show Himself strong on your behalf.

Free yourself today by letting the All-Powerful, Sovereign and Faithful God do what He does best. He is an Expert Fighter, who has never lost a battle.

Pray to God today, tell Him about your battles, and share with Him how much you trust and desperately need Him. God already knows, but He wants you to express it to Him instead of everyone else. God is waiting for you right now.

Practical Application for Kingdom Living

Write down every battle you have been dealing with, and then begin to pray to God every day until he gives you the victory over each and every one of them.

Kingdom Principles for Everyday Living

Day 27

Creating Wealth is Not a Mystery

Give, and [gifts] will be given to you; good measure, pressed down, shaken together, and running over, will they pour into [the pouch formed by] the bosom [of your robe and used as a bag]. For with the measure you deal out [with the measure you use when you confer benefit is on others], it will be measured back to you.
(Luke 6:38 AMP)

If you think education is expensive, wait until you see how expensive stupidity can be! God wants us to be the lender and not the borrower. Being a borrower creates debt and soon debt will become your master, which makes you a slave to money. God called all of us to make wise decisions concerning money. He wants us to own assets and not liabilities. When you loan money and you make a return, you create an asset. However, if you borrow money and you do not make a return on your money, you have created a liability.

When you give to the Kingdom of God, you are making a deposit, which is a sure way to generate a return. This is called creating a spiritual asset. What are you investing in? There is no better investment than the Kingdom of God because you are guaranteed a return that is above and beyond your expectations.

Now to Him who is able to do exceedingly abundantly above all that we ask or think, according to the power that works in us. (Ephesians 3:20 KJV)

Practical Application for Kingdom Living

How will you invest in the Kingdom today? Write down to whom or where God wants you to sow. Hurry and plant your seed, so He can generate your return.

Day 28

God is Everything

The LORD is my rock, my fortress, and my savior; my God is my rock, in whom I find protection. He is my shield, the power that saves me, and my place of safety. (Psalm 18:2 NLT)

Do you need strength today? Perhaps you need someone who can deliver you from all of life's dilemmas. Maybe you placed your trust in man, only to be let down. Maybe you said, "I will never trust anyone again."

There are countless people hurting today just like you. Perhaps someone has injured you and now you are deeply wounded. I hear you saying, "I will never let anyone get that close to me again." Every time someone gets close to you, you have a tendency to build walls, set barriers in place, along with certain other defense mechanisms to protect your heart.

God wants to heal and deliver you from all your past hurts, sufferings and pains. God says, "You can trust Me. I will not hurt you. I will be your strength and protector." Who would not serve a God like this? He is all you need.

Tell God today whatever it is that has hurt you. He does not want you to be in bondage any longer. When Christ died for you, He paid the price for everything and that includes your freedom.

So if the Son sets you free, you are truly free. (John 8:36 KJV)

Practical Application for Kingdom Living

Take a few moments to write down all the times people have hurt you in your life. Begin to pray to our Heavenly Father and ask Him to remove your scars and heal your broken heart. Tell God you want to be whole again and you want Him to put all the broken pieces back together.

Day 29

Comfort During Your Time of Mourning

All praise to God, the Father of our Lord Jesus Christ. God is our merciful Father and the source of all Comfort. (2 Corinthians 1:3 NLT)

Losing a loved one can be difficult. No matter how prepared we think we are for death, we are not. Everyone mourns in their own way. When the time comes, we may find ourselves deeply hurting. It does not matter how strong we may be, our pain may seem unbearable. Even though we try our best to take it to God, we may still feel a huge void in our hearts. Mourning is part of the process. As we trust God, He heals every broken place.

Today God wants to comfort you during your time of mourning. As God begins to heal your broken heart, meditate on these comforting Psalms throughout the day.

The LORD is my rock and my fortress and my deliverer, My God, my rock, in whom I take refuge; My shield and the horn of my salvation, my stronghold (Psalm 18:2 KJV).

This is my comfort in my affliction, that Thy word has revived me (Psalm 119:50 KJV).

For Thou dost light my lamp; The LORD my God illumines my darkness (Psalm 18:28 KJV).

Even though I walk through the valley of the shadow of death, I fear no evil; for Thou art with me; Thy rod and Thy staff, they comfort me (Psalm 23:4 KJV).

My flesh and my heart may fail, but God is the strength of my heart and my portion forever (Psalm 73:26 KJV).

Practical Application for Kingdom Living

I suggest every morning when you wake up and before you go to bed, take some time and meditate on the previously mentioned Psalms. Each time you do this, ask God to comfort your heart during this time of and every one of them.

Kingdom Principles for Everyday Living

Day 30

Your Greatest Weapon is Love

If I could speak all the languages of earth and of angels, but did not love others, I would only be a noisy gong or a clanging cymbal.
(1 Corinthians 13:1 NLT)

Love is the only thing in the universe that will never fail. As the Psalmist wrote, *"my flesh and my heart may fail, but God is the Rock and firm strength of my heart and my Portion forever"* (Psalm 73:26 AMP). When love abounds, the end result is God is revealed in every area of our lives. Love is the foundational element—it has meaning and substance. Love contains the power to transform circumstances and most of all hearts.

Love is the only weapon that is both offensive and defensive. It always believes, never doubts, keeps no record of wrongdoing, always retains hope, quickly forgives and releases payments and debts. Love is full of good.

Love overcomes and conquers evil with good. *"Do not fight evil with evil, but overcome evil with good." (see Romans 12:17)* Love remains and refuses to move out of the character of God. It takes love to pray for those who persecute you, and it takes a real child of God to love your enemies.

Today, pray for your enemies and thank God for them. If it were not for your enemies, you would not be where you are today. Your enemies are the ones who have pushed and stretched you to your limit, compelling you to want to succeed.

It took extreme pressure, adverse situations and tight places to reveal your capabilities. If it were not for all the resistance and opposition in life, you would not know God's ability to deliver you and promote you to your God-given purpose.

Today, praise God for each and every one of your enemies! Pray for them and love them the way Christ loves you.

Practical Application for Kingdom Living

Take a few moments to write down all the times people have hurt you in your life. Ask God to teach you how to Love them unconditionally, until you no longer have resentment, bitterness and unforgiveness in your heart.

Kingdom Principles for Everyday Living

Day 31

What is Salvation?

And now you Gentiles have also heard the truth, the Good News that God saves you. And when you believed in Christ, He identified you as His own by giving you the Holy Spirit, whom He promised long ago. (Ephesians 1:13 NLT)

Salvation is the act of saving or protecting someone from harm, risk, loss, and destruction. Salvation is one of the promises of God to all believers for eligibility for the gift of eternal life. In the full sense of the word, to be "saved" means to have received eternal life.

The word salvation is also used to describe the process we go through before we can receive eternal life. Several scriptures characterize the word "saved" as redemption—one of the steps in the process of salvation.

And you also were included in Christ when you heard the Word of truth, the gospel of your salvation. Having believed, you were marked in Him with a seal, the promised Holy Spirit. (Ephesians 1:13).

The Bible says, we have been bought with the precious blood of Jesus and we have been sealed with the Holy Spirit.

Practical Application for Kingdom Living

Write down some specific things that have impacted your life concerning the Bible and then ask God to help you use those things as ministering tools to glorify God.

_____
_____
_____
_____
_____
_____
_____
_____
_____
_____
_____
_____
_____
_____
_____
_____
_____
_____
_____
_____
_____

Day 32

Faith Being Tested

Faith is the confidence that what we hope for will actually happen; it gives us assurance about things we cannot see. (Hebrews 11:1 NLT)

More and more, life seems to present some pretty stressful tests. Without fail, our faith is being tested. The Bible says, *"Faith is the substance of things hoped for and the evidence of things not seen (Hebrews 11:1 KJV).* Faith is not faith unless it is being tested. Regardless of how difficult life is, we have to look past what we see and feel, and choose to believe God. We must hold on to the substance of hope. How can we have trust in something not seen? It is only evidence when we can see it, right? Wrong!

In comparison to the world's standard, everything is reversed in the Kingdom of God. We have to disconnect ourselves from our emotions and what we can see. We have to start looking through the lenses of the Spirit and not our circumstances.

Without spending time with God, it is impossible to hear from God. As you pray, fast, and study the Word of God, start asking Him the hard questions concerning your life. Years ago, I inquired of Him, "If You are who You say You are, then I need You to show up in my life today in a MAJOR way!" Because He is faithful, He responded. Do not think for one minute that God is not concerned about you. God is mindful of every detail concerning your life and He is waiting for you to have a dialogue with Him right now.

Let me leave this with you: The Bible says, *"Do not get weary in well doing for if you faint not* (which means do not give up) *you shall reap in due season (Galatians 6:9 KJV).*

Do not give up. It might be tough, but God will reward your faithfulness. God just wants your participation. You can make it. I believe in you, and this too shall pass. Much love to you, as you experience your new faith walk today.

Practical Application for Kingdom Living

List the major areas in your life, where you need to exercise your faith. Pray to God and ask Him to help you increase your faith according to *Hebrews 11:1*.

Kingdom Principles for Everyday Living

Day 33

Who are You?

> *When Jesus came to the region of Caesarea Philippi, he asked his disciples, "Who do people say that the Son of Man is?" "Well," they replied, "some say John the Baptist, some say Elijah, and others say Jeremiah or one of the other prophets." Then he asked them, "But who do you say I am?" (Matthew 16:13-15 MSG)*

What is your true identity? I did not ask you what your mother named you. I did not ask you what people call you, I asked, "who are you?" I am not asking you about the title you hold on your job, nor about the position you hold at your church. I am asking you, "Who are you?"

We have been so caught up in other identities; we have forgotten who we are. If I ask you who are you, you may say, "I am Elder Doorknob, Minister So Much, Executive Phillip My Pockets, or Administrator Got It Going-on." Nevertheless, the question still remains, "Who are you?"

Jesus asked the disciples, "*...Who do men say that I am" (see Matthew 16:13)*? And they began to give Him all kinds of names. Although they had been with Him for quite some time, they still did not know who He truly was.

If you do not know who your Heavenly Father is, then chances are you do not know who you are. It was Peter that spoke up and said, "*You are the Christ, the Messiah—the Son of the living God.* Peter realized it, but not without the aid of the Holy Spirit. It takes God to give you your true identity in Him. So, I will ask the question again, "Who are you?"

Practical Application for Kingdom Living

Take some time to pray to God and ask Him who you are. When He begins to reveal to you who you are, write it down. Now is the time to step out and start being who God created you to be.

Day 34

A Healthy Body and a Prosperous Soul

> *But now the righteousness of God has been revealed independently and altogether apart from the Law, although actually it is attested by the Law and the Prophets. (Romans 3:21 AMP)*

There are people who have lived empty lives, never knowing what life had to offer them. God has fixed it so we cannot live without Him. God started with the Law, knowing we could never fulfill it.

The Law was only to show us how messed up we were. The Law was never intended to be a permanent solution, but a temporary solution. It was legalistic and left no room for error. The Law showed neither grace nor mercy to those who violated it. It only showed judgment. The Law was only a precursor to a structured life. This held true until the real Sacrificial Lamb, Jesus Christ, the Giver of Life, arrived on the scene.

According to Scriptures, a priest went into the Holy of Holies once a year to take a lamb to slay to atone for the sins of God's people. The priest would sacrifice lambs, bullocks, and pigeons, but there was only one true Sacrificial Lamb and His name was Jesus Christ.

You see, before we met Jesus, we were helpless. When we met Jesus, we become powerful. When the dunamis (a Greek word meaning dynamite) power came into our lives, we became an effective witness for Jesus. The Bible says, *"I am not ashamed of the Gospel for it is the power of God unto salvation to everyone who believes..."* In order to have a healthy body and a prosperous soul, we need the power of God in our lives (*Romans 1:16 KJV*).

Practical Application for Kingdom Living

List five areas in your life where you know you need power. Then ask God to transfer His power into your life, so you can live a purpose driven life.

_____
_____
_____
_____
_____
_____
_____
_____
_____
_____
_____
_____
_____
_____
_____
_____
_____

Day 35

Do not Blame God

Better to be poor and honest, than to be dishonest and a fool. Enthusiasm without knowledge is no good; haste makes mistakes. People ruin their lives by their own foolishness and then are angry at the LORD. (Proverbs 19:1-3 NLT)

It is interesting to know people live double lives. They say they love God, but their hearts are far from Him. How is it that in most cities we have churches on every corner and we still lack the power to change our neighborhoods? In order to survive the crucial days we are living in, we need the knowledge and power of God.

If we make decisions apart from God, when everything fails, we cannot blame Him. It doesn't matter how much money we may have if we are dishonest and ignorant of God's Kingdom Principles.

The only way we can have sound knowledge is by being connected to God. If we operate outside of the knowledge of God, it will cause us to make numerous mistakes in life.

The scriptures are clear in telling us what we need to do in order to stay connected to the Kingdom of God. The Bible instructs us to be honest and knowledgeable concerning the things of God. Therefore, if we choose to use an alternative route, then we cannot blame God when we experience devastating loss.

Scores of people have ruined their lives due to the lack of knowledge and foolishness. These same people often blame God. You must be real with God because if you are a counterfeit, He knows. Today, start being honest with God and pray for His wisdom. The Bible says, *"If any of you lacks wisdom, let him ask of God, who gives to all liberally" (James 1:5 KJV)*. God wants to share His wisdom with you, but you have to ask.

God knows our heart and has given us an allotment of mercy and grace for all our mistakes. However, we must strive to maintain our integrity and honesty as we constantly seek the wisdom of God in all things.

Practical Application for Kingdom Living

Meditate on *Proverbs 19:1-3*, and then pray to God and ask Him for His divine honesty, wisdom, and knowledge, so you can receive everything God has in store for you.

Kingdom Principles for Everyday Living

Day 36

Give God Praise and Rejoice

O God, whom I praise, do not stand silent and aloof while the wicked slander me and tell lies about me. They surround me with hateful words and fight against me for no reason. I love them, but they try to destroy me with accusations even as I am praying for them! They repay evil for good, and hatred for my love. They say, "Get an evil person to turn against him. Send an accuser to bring him to trial."
(Psalm 109:1-6, 21, 26-31 NLT)

Have you ever done the right thing while evil people kept doing wrong toward you? You know you could easily go "51/50" on them, but instead, you pray for them, only to be attacked by them again and again. If you can relate to what I am saying, then I would like to encourage you to read *Psalm 109*.

King David was praying to God and was saying, "God. I am praising You, but do not just stand there and let them do whatever they want to do to me. God, You see everything, so why are You allowing this to happen to me? I know You see the false accusations toward me and You know they are not true, but yet You remain silent. I try to love them despite how they treat me, but they continuously attack me." No matter what, as Christians, we have to remain the same.

This is what I enjoy the most about King David. He did not run from God, but he ran toward Him: He said, "O Sovereign God, Your reputation is on the line, so rescue me. Not because of me, but because You are faithful and good." Have you ever talked to God like this and asked Him to deliver you from your enemies by saying, "God let my enemies understand my deliverance is Your doing, and not me. It is only You who can deliver me from the hands of my enemy." King David said it like this, "Regardless of what it looks like, I still trust You. They can curse me if they like, but I know You are still going to bless me." When dealing with foolish people, this Psalm will get you through every time.

Practical Application for Kingdom Living

Take the time and meditate on this scripture. As you deal with those who come against you, ask God to strengthen your faith and help you maintain a right attitude.

Kingdom Principles for Everyday Living

Day 37

You Have Been Chosen by God

And the Lord said to satan, Have you considered My servant Job, that there is none like him on the earth, a blameless and upright man, one who [reverently] fears God and abstains from and shuns evil [because it is wrong]? (Job 1:8 AMP)

Why is it always me God? What have I done to deserve this? God, what else must I do in order for You to move in my life? Have you ever pleaded with God and asked Him these questions?

Sometimes it has nothing to do with you or how much you have messed up in life. It has everything to do with God. He wants to use your deliverance from those experiences for His glory.

If God did not know you had the shoulders to bare these heavy burdens, He would not have allowed you to be selected for a time such as this. You have been singled out and handpicked by God. God knew you had everything you would ever need to conquer your journey of adversity and pain.

There are "Kingdom Principles" in the Word of God, and in these Kingdom Principles, God gives us instructions on how to live a Kingdom Lifestyle. Whenever you live according to these Kingdom Principles, you receive Kingdom benefits. It is up to you to read His Word and understand your benefits. As you align your life according to His will, take God's Word at face value, apply His Word to your life, and believe what God says will surely come to pass.

Kingdom Principles for Everyday Living

When you are in the will of God and living according to the Word of God, this gives you the right to place a demand on the things of God. Some times you can place a demand on God and not see anything, because placing a demand on God doesn't overrule the timing of God.

Have you ever looked at your life and asked the question, "Why me?" In those times, God may say, "Why not you? I have given you everything you need. However, the process I am taking you through is not for you, but for someone else." Can you be a blessing to someone else based on the journey God has allowed you to go through? Can you press through your pain and begin to humble yourself before God Almighty?

> *Job 13:15 (AMP) "Though He slay me, yet will I wait for and trust Him and behold, He will slay me; I have no hope—nevertheless, I will maintain and argue my ways before Him and even to His face."*

Your assignment is not always for you. God can use your assignment for His glory and to bless others.

Practical Application for Kingdom Living

What are you going through that makes no sense to you? Write those things down. Continue to persevere and trust God and believe that *"...all things work together for your good..." (see Romans 8:28).*

Day 38

Are You Really Born Again?

You search the Scriptures because you think they give you eternal life. But the Scriptures point to me! Yet you refuse to come to me to receive this life. Your approval means nothing to me, because I know you do not have God's love within you. For I have come to you in my Father's name, and you have rejected me. Yet, if others come in their own name, you gladly welcome them. No wonder you cannot believe! For you gladly honor each other, but you do not care about the honor that comes from the one who alone is God.
(John 5:39-44 NLT)

We all have our own idea of what it means to be saved. Sometimes we really do not want to hear the truth. If you ask most people, I am almost certain most feel they are saved. But, the real question is, are you born again?

During my trip to the Holy Land, Israel, I met a middle-aged man who had attended church all of his life, but had never really confessed Jesus Christ as his Lord and Savior. Sadly, it was not until he was on this trip that he found out that he was not born again.

Just because you go to church does not mean you are born again. It is a terrible thing to climb a ladder all of your life only to find out you have been climbing the wrong ladder!

To be born again is as easy as ABC: A̲ccept, B̲elieve, and C̲onfess.

- You must **accept** Jesus Christ into your heart

- **Believe** that Jesus Christ died on the cross for your sins
- **Confess** with your mouth that He is the Lord of your life

Some people's concept of being saved is totally opposite to what the Bible says. However, John makes it clear in *John 5* as to why everyone is not saved. The Bible also says, *"I am the way, the truth, and the life, and no one comes to the Father except through me"* (John 14:6)

It cannot get any clearer than that. If you did not know before, you know now.

Practical Application for Kingdom Living

Have you ever committed your life to the Lord? If you have not, I suggest you go back to the previous page and repeat the "ABC" steps to the Lord. Once you do these steps, you receive eternal life immediately, and you are now born again. Now go and find a local church where you can grow and learn how to live according to the decision that you just made. Welcome to the Kingdom of God.

Kingdom Principles for Everyday Living

Day 39

Get in the Game

Athletes work hard and are disciplined in their training. They know that if they win games, they will win the prize. They do not think about a prize that may fade away someday. Christians work hard and are disciplined as well, but they do so to win an eternal prize. (1 Corinthians 9:25 NLT)

Do you feel like you are sitting on the bench of life with great skills, but you cannot get into the game? Politics, favoritism or something else may be the reason you are on the bench. You may be certain those playing in the game do not exhibit your skills, but the fact remains, they are in the game and you are not.

I remember a conversation I had with my best friend regarding the topic. We were talking about life and how unfair it can be at times. During the conversation, God gave me a revelation.

Take the time to reflect on how much time you may have wasted sitting on the bench in some area of your life. While you are sitting on the bench and others are in the game, I want you to know, you are only on the bench temporarily. God knows your perspective from the bench differs from the perspective of those playing in the game.

If you are sitting on the bench, instead of complaining, realize that because of your perfect view of the game, you are acquiring wisdom for your life. You can see all the mistakes and the errors the players are making. You can also see the cause of the turnovers that are occurring. Maybe it is not such a bad thing to be where you are right now. Every time you hear the coach screaming and yelling at the team concerning what they are not doing right, you can make a mental note for future reference. I hear you saying, "When I get in the game, I am not going to make the same mistakes."

Likewise, when you went to college or received specific training in your field, it was not in vain or a waste of time. Preparation is never wasted time. You see people with the same degree and less experience and training than you, playing in the game and constantly making error after error. This is an opportunity for you to shine.

Now is the time to prepare or revamp your business plan. Begin drafting your business plan using all of the information you gathered while watching others. This is what is going to make you money.

Today, start telling yourself, "When I get in the game, I will be prepared to stay in the game. I am never going to come out of the game." You have to encourage yourself by saying, "I am in it to win it, and I am going to be the best in the game!" You may have been watching for a long time from the outside. Now you are ready to win the game called life from the inside.

When the coach calls your name to get in the game, are you going to be ready or are you going to repeat the same turnovers and mistakes you watched others make over and over again? Now is the time to make a change and get in the game!

Practical Application for Kingdom Living

What do you need to do in order to get in the game? Write those things down. Ask God to order your steps, give you wisdom, and an opportunity to get in the game.

Kingdom Principles for Everyday Living

Day 40

Turning Toward God

> *Yet I am glad now, not because you were pained, but because you were pained into repentance [and so turned back to God]; for you felt a grief such as God meant you to feel, so that in nothing you might suffer loss through us or harm for what we did.*
> *(2 Corinthians 7:9 AMP)*

We cannot continue to live a life of sin and still expect God to show up. Sin separates us from God. Therefore, the first thing we need to do is to be honest with ourselves and then with God. If we want change in our lives, then we need to turn our hearts toward God.

Doing the same thing every day and looking for different results is called insanity. We should repent to God for all the times we have missed the mark and fallen short of His glory.

Repenting is not for God; it is for us. Let us turn our lives around and bend our hearts toward our Sovereign God. Let God cleanse us with the blood of Christ from all of our unrighteousness. Let us begin to create an atmosphere where we can dwell with Him

> *Yet I am glad now, not because you were pained, but because you were pained into repentance [and so turned back to God]; for you felt a grief such as God meant you to feel, so that in nothing you might suffer loss through us or harm for what we did*
> *(2 Corinthians 7:9 AMP).*
>
> *If we confess our sins, He is faithful and just to forgive us [our] sins, and to cleanse us from all unrighteousness* (1 John 1:9 KJV).

Today can be your new day with a new beginning, but it all begins with turning to God, and total repentance.

Practical Application for Kingdom Living

Take a few moments and write down the things you need to repent to God for. Once you have written those things down, pray to God according to *(1 John 1:9)*.

Kingdom Principles for Everyday Living

www.ingramcontent.com/pod-product-compliance
Lightning Source LLC
LaVergne TN
LVHW052255070426
835507LV00035B/2912